Authentic Freedom

Claiming a Life of Contentment and Joy

Student Workbook©

> *"I will lead you out of the land of slavery to a land of freedom*
> *— a good and gracious land flowing with milk and honey."*
>
> Exodus 3:8

Lauri Ann Lumby

Authentic Freedom Press
Oshkosh, Wisconsin

Authentic Freedom Press

Published in the United States of America
by Authentic Freedom Press
Oshkosh, Wisconsin
http://www.yourspiritualtruth.com

Interior design and composition by Sandi Carpenter
Cover design by Gretchen Herrmann, Primary Colors

ISBN – 13: 978-1478396611
ISBN – 10: 147839661X

Manufactured in the United States of America

CONTENTS

A Note from the Author

Authentic Freedom – Claiming a Life of Contentment and Joy is a journey of self-discovery and transformation. Through this process, you will begin to become aware of the many ways in which you are imprisoned by fear, false perceptions and illusions – and how these fears and false-perceptions stand in the way of achieving authentic freedom. Authentic freedom is recognized by a life in which you know the consistent experience of peace and where you are free to openly share the gifts that God gave you. Authentic freedom is your Divine inheritance, and the way that God intends you to live. Instead of embracing this Divine inheritance, most of us are left to struggle through our lives, plagued by the irrational fears, anxieties and compulsions that hold us prisoner.

The Authentic Freedom Course gives you a map to this freedom. Hidden within Jesus' teachings and ministry is the *core truth* that Jesus came to reveal. This is the truth that Jesus promised as "the truth that shall set you free." It is in living this truth that we experience a life of authentic freedom. Unfortunately, most of us do not have access to this truth. Instead, we suffer from the *core spiritual wound* which results in the *seven core fears* and their resulting compulsions. Fortunately, out of his deep love and compassion, Jesus left behind a myriad of tools to help us to be healed of the core wound and its resulting fears so that we can once again enjoy the fullness of joy. Jesus' teachings can all be boiled down to this one core truth. Getting to this truth however is not that simple.

The *seven sacred truths* provide the path through which realization of the core truth is made possible. In learning to embrace these seven sacred truths, our core spiritual wound, along with the resulting spiritual fears can once and for all find healing and release.

Entering into the process of **Authentic Freedom**, you will discover a powerful tool for healing and transformation. Through scripture, an introduction into Eastern Energy Medicine, explanation of the Authentic Freedom concepts, and practical exercises in meditation and contemplation, you will have an opportunity to integrate this knowledge into your own life experience. With diligent practice and through the gift of Grace, you will experience the expansive freedom of being released from the fears and compulsions which have held you prisoner within yourself. Freed from these obstacles, you will once again be able to live fully in the peace and joy of who God made you to be. Through this liberation, your own unique giftedness will be able to emerge and you will discover the excitement of being able to generously share your gifts in the world. In this way, you shall become a vessel through which God's transforming love and compassion will be released in our world. Many blessings to you as you discover for yourself the land of freedom – **the good and gracious land, flowing with milk and honey**.

Lauri Lumby
Authentic Freedom Ministries
http://yourspiritualtruth.com

SESSION ONE

The Road to Freedom

The Lord said, I have witnessed the affliction of my people and have heard their cry of complaint, so I know well that they are suffering. Therefore I have come to lead them out of the land of slavery, into a good and gracious land, a land flowing with milk and honey.

Exodus 3:8

And you will know the truth and the truth shall set you free.

John 8:32

SPIRITUAL PRACTICE

You are invited to prayerfully read through the scripture passages above. Choose the scripture passage that speaks to you the most, then look for a word or a phrase that jumps out at you. Use that phrase as a mantra, repeating it over and over in your mind, allowing it to help move you into a prayerful and meditative state. Allow yourself to rest in this space for 15-20 minutes. When your mind wanders, return to the mantra phrase. Allow your mind to flow, inviting images and reflections to come. Record any thoughts or reflections below and on the next page. Then, answer the reflection question at the bottom of the following page.

Reflection Question:

What does "Authentic Freedom" mean to you?

THE ROAD TO FREEDOM

Fear	Compulsion	Seven Chakras	Truth	Virtue
There is not enough	Gluttony	Root	God meets all of my needs in abundance	Temperance/ Faith
I will not be able to bring forth life that will persist	Lust	Sacral	I am uniquely gifted to bring forth creative life so that God's love may be revealed	Fortitude
I can't	Wrath	Solar Plexus	It is only those things within me that keep me from being and living as my most authentic self.	Mercy
I am not loved	Envy	Heart	Love is my true nature and cannot be denied or taken away	Compassion/ Love
I am unable to express my truth	Greed	Throat	Expressing my truth shall set me free	Generosity
I do not know	Sloth	Brow	I am One with the Source of truth through my Oneness with God. This is where truth is revealed	Zeal
I am alone	Pride	Crown	I am One with God and therefore One with all that is	Humility

HOMEWORK ASSIGNMENT SESSION ONE:

In the coming week, be aware of situations, responses and actions in your life that may indicate a lack of freedom. Where do you find yourself indulging the following fears:

- **There is not enough**

- **I will not be able to bring forth life that will persist**

- **I can't**

- **I am not loved**

- **I am unable to express my truth**

- **I do not know**

- **I am alone**

SESSION TWO

The Core Wound – Healing the Separation

And you will know the truth and the truth shall set you free.

John 8:32

Consecrate them in the truth. Your word is truth. As you sent me into the world, so I sent them into the world. And I consecrate myself for them, so that they may be consecrated in truth. I pray not only for them, but also for those who will believe in me through their word, so that they may all be one, as you, Father, are in me and I in you, that they also may be in us, that the world may believe that you sent me. And I have given them the glory you gave me, so that they may be one, as we are one, I in them and you in me, that they may be brought into perfection as one, that the world may know that you sent me, and that you loved them even as you loved me.

John 17:17-23

SPIRITUAL PRACTICE

You are invited to prayerfully reflect on the scripture passages on the previous page. Read it through several times, slowly, meditatively, allowing the words to move deeply into your being. Look for a particular word or phrase that seems to speak to you and spend time repeating that word or phrase, allowing it to move more and more deeply into your being. Allow this word or phrase to be God's word for you today, nourishing, strengthening and challenging you. Record any thoughts or reflections in the space provided.

SESSION THREE

Abundance Is Yours

Fear **There is not enough**
Compulsion **Gluttony**
Truth **God meets my needs in abundance**

For I know well the plans I have in mind for you, said the Lord, plans for prosperity, not for woe.

Jeremiah 29:11

Therefore I tell you, do not worry about your life, what you will eat (or drink), or about your body, what you will wear. Is not life more than food and the body more than clothing? Look at the birds in the sky; they do not sow or reap, they gather nothing into barns, yet our Creator feeds them. Are not you more important than they?

Matthew 6:25-26

SPIRITUAL PRACTICE

Take a few minutes to prayerfully read through the scripture passages on the previous page. Allow yourself to absorb the message of these passages. Is there a specific word or phrase that jumps out at you? Repeat that word or phrase over and over in your mind as a mantra. Allow this phrase to help you to move into a more deeply meditative state. Just be with that word or phrase for 15-20 minutes. What thoughts or reflections arise? Record them below:

ABUNDANCE

Fear There is not enough

Compulsion Gluttony

Sacred Truth Your Divine Source meets all of your needs in abundance

Chakra Root

How we experience this fear being indulged

Emotions Fear, insecurity, restlessness, ungroundedness.

Behaviors Compulsive spending, buying, collecting, consumerism, wastefulness, self-deprivation, over and under eating.

Physical Weight problems (too much, too little), eating disorders, leg, knees, feet problems, constipation, hemorrhoids, sciatica, difficulty bringing ideas, dreams, visions into reality. Adrenal disorders. Problems with teeth, bones, large intestines, colon.

Element Earth

Evidence of Healing

Inner State Stillness, security, stability, faith and trust, ability to bring dreams into reality.

Virtue Temperance

Grace Peace

QUESTIONS FOR FURTHER REFLECTION

❶ Do you believe that your needs (for food, shelter, clothing, love, support, nurturing, time, resources) will be abundantly met? If not, why?

❷ How is this fear currently manifesting in your life (lower back pain, fear, lack of focus, inability to complete projects, feelings of insecurity, etc.)

❸ What benefit(s) do you receive from believing this fear? (ie: "it allows me to receive sympathy from others.")

❹ How would your life change if you believed that your needs would be met?

❺ Why wouldn't you decide TODAY to embrace the truth of abundance?

❻ What do you need RIGHT NOW to believe this truth? Ask your higher power RIGHT NOW to help you to receive that which you perceive you will need in order to believe the truth of abundance! Write your request below.

SESSION FOUR

You Are Uniquely Gifted

The Fear	I am not able to bring forth life that will persist
Compulsion	Lust
Truth	I am uniquely gifted to bring forth creative life so that God's love may be revealed

This is how it is with the kingdom of God; it is as if a man were to scatter seed on the land and would sleep and rise night and day and the seed would sprout and grow, he knows not how. Of its own accord the land yields fruit, first the blade, then the ear, then the full grain in the ear. And when the grain is ripe, he wields the sickle at once, for the harvest has come.

Mark 4: 26-29

Thus says the Lord: Just as from the heavens the rain and snow come down and do not return there until they have watered the earth, making it fertile and fruitful, giving seed to the one who sows and bread to the one who eats, so shall my word be that goes forth from my mouth; It shall not return to me void, but shall do my will, achieving the end for which I sent it.

Isaiah 55: 10-11

SPIRITUAL PRACTICE #1

Prayerfully read through the scripture passages on the previous page and reflect on:

❶ The mystery of a seed's growth

❷ The fulfillment of God's will

Reflect on how these stories might bear meaning in your own life. Record your reflections in the space provided.

SPIRITUAL PRACTICE #2

You are invited to participate in an exercise in "Imagination-Contemplation". This prayer form, popularized by St. Ignatius of Loyola, is an opportunity to allow our Divine Source to communicate with us through our imagination. Prayerfully read and re-read the story from Exodus below, allowing the story to sink into your being. Choose a character from the story and imagine that you are that character. Recreate the story in your mind living-out the role of the character you have chosen. Envision the scene in great detail. What is the environment like, the weather, the smells and the scenery around you? What are the emotions that are surfacing as you find yourself immersed in the story as it unfolds in your imagination? Allow your creative mind the freedom to take you where you need to go. Spend 20 minutes or more in this activity and record your reflections in the space provided.

Moses – drawn from the water

Pharaoh then commanded all his subjects, "Throw into the river every boy that is born to the Hebrews, but you may let all the girls live."

Now a certain man of the house of Levi married a Levite woman, who conceived and bore a son. Seeing that he was a goodly child, she hid him for three months. When she could hide him no longer, she took a papyrus basket, daubed it with bitumen and pitch, and putting the child in it, placed it among the reeds on the river bank. His sister stationed herself at a distance to find out what would happen to him.

Pharaoh's daughter came down to the river to bathe, while her maids walked along the river bank. Noticing the basket among the reeds, she sent her handmaid to fetch it. On opening it, she looked and lo, there was a baby boy, crying! She was moved with pity for him and said, "It is one of the Hebrew's children." Then his sister asked Pharaoh's daughter, "Shall I go and call one of the Hebrew women to nurse the child for you?" "Yes, do so," she answered. So the maiden went and called the child's own mother. Pharaoh's daughter said to her, "Take this child and nurse it for me, and I will repay you." The woman therefore took the child and nursed it. Then the child grew, she brought him to Pharaoh's daughter, who adopted him as her son and called him Moses; for she said, "I drew him out of the water."

Exodus 1: 22; 2: 1-10

YOU ARE UNIQUELY GIFTED

Fear   I will be unable to bring forth life that will persist

Compulsion   Lust

Sacred Truth   You are co-creator with God and when you surrender to this process, together you bring forth life that persists.

Chakra   Sacral

How we experience this fear being indulged

Emotions   Desperation, powerlessness.

Behaviors   Abuse of power or being abused by power, addictions, co-dependency, lack of boundaries, unhealthy sexual behaviors and compulsions, not expressing the life within us.

Physical   Impotence, frigidity, uterine, bladder or kidney trouble, stiff lower back, reproductive organ issues, prostate cancer; uterine, ovarian, cervical cancers.

Chakra   Sacral Plexus

Element   Water

Evidence of healing

Inner State   Balanced emotions, ability to "let go", healthy intimate relationships, creativity

Virtue   Fortitude

Grace   Contentment

QUESTIONS FOR FURTHER REFLECTION

❶ Do you believe that you are uniquely gifted to bring forth creative life? If not, why?

❷ How is this fear currently manifest in your life (reproductive organ issues, bladder or kidney problems, depression, issues of co-dependency, etc.)

❸ What benefit(s) do you receive from believing this fear? (ie: "It allows me to receive sympathy from others.")

❹ How would your life change if you did believe that you were uniquely gifted to reveal God's love in the world?

❺ Why wouldn't you decide TODAY to embrace the truth of your unique giftedness?

❻ What do you need RIGHT NOW to believe this truth? Ask your higher power RIGHT NOW to help you to receive that which you perceive you will need in order to believe the truth of your unique giftedness.   Write your request below.

SESSION FIVE

You Can Do It

Fear	**I can't**
Compulsion	**Wrath**
Promise	**It is only those things within me (fear, resentment, anger, etc.) that prevent me from being and living as my most authentic self. (The highest vision of myself that God has imagined!)**

In the year king Uzziah died, I saw the Lord seated on a high and lofty throne, with the train of his garment filling the temple.

Then I said, "Woe is me, I am doomed! For I am a man of unclean lips, living among a people of unclean lips; yet my eyes have seen the King, the Lord of hosts!" Then one of the seraphim flew to me, holding an ember which he had taken with tongs from the altar.

He touched my mouth with it. "See," he said, "now that this has touched your lips, your wickedness is removed, your sin purged."

Then I heard the voice of the Lord saying, "Whom shall I send? Who will go for us?" "Here I am;" I said, "send me!" And he replied, "Go..."

Isaiah 6: 1, 5-9

SPIRITUAL PRACTICE

Part One: Brainstorming

You will need 20 minutes for this part of the activity. You might want to set a kitchen timer and have extra paper ready....just in case. Sit down with this workbook and a pen and in the space provided begin to write, **I can't**. Write **I can't I can't I can't** over and over and over until your creative mind starts to fill in the blanks. Keep writing down all the areas in your life where you currently believe the fear **I can't**. If you run out of ideas, just keep writing **I can't**. The purpose of this exercise is to free the most vulnerable and hidden fears of "I can't" that are hiding behind all the other distracting fears. Write for the entire 20 minutes then complete the visualization exercise that follows.

Part Two – Visualization

After you have completed the brainstorming session, place yourself in the reading from **Isaiah**. Imagine that you, like Isaiah, desire to be free of the inner obstacles to being and living as your most authentic self, the person God created you to be. Bring to mind all of the "I can'ts" that surfaced in the brainstorming exercise. Then imagine the seraphim coming to you with the burning ember and bringing the ember to your lips, cleansing and purging you of that fear. Imagine the ember brought to your lips over and over and over as your fear is released and purged. Record any thoughts or feelings below:

YOU CAN DO IT

Fear   I can't

Compulsion   Wrath

Sacred Truth There is nothing outside of you that can keep you from living freely as your most authentic self – the person God has made you to be.

Chakra   Solar Plexus

How we experience this fear being indulged

Emotions   Anger, rage, resentment, paralysis, impatience, irritability.

Behaviors   Projecting, lashing out, building resentments, unhealthy expressions of anger, depression (anger turned inward), worry

Physical   Ulcer, diabetes, hypoglycemia, digestive disorders, liver and gallbladder issues, immune system disorders, pancreas, spleen.

Element   Fire

Evidence of healing

Inner state   Laughter, joy, self-esteem, willpower, forgiveness

Virtue   Mercy

Grace   Empowerment

QUESTIONS FOR FURTHER REFLECTION

❶ What are the things within that are currently preventing you from living and being your most authentic self?

❷ How are these areas of resistance currently manifest in your life (ulcers, blood sugar problems, rage and anger, migraine headaches, depression, acid reflux, obsessive worry, low self-image, lack of self-confidence, lack of courage or bravery, etc.)?

❸ What benefit(s) do you receive from not living as your most authentic self? (ie: "It allows me to receive sympathy from others.")

❹ How would your life change if you were able to be your most authentic self?

❺ Why wouldn't you decide TODAY to embrace the truth of Authentic Freedom?

❻ What do you need RIGHT NOW to believe this truth? Ask your higher power RIGHT NOW to help you to receive that which you perceive you will need in order to believe the truth of your ability to be and live as your most authentic self! Write your request below.

SESSION SIX

Love Is Who You Are

The Fear	**I will not be loved**
Compulsion	**Envy**
Truth	**Love is the very essence of who you are and therefore cannot be denied nor does it need to be earned.**

But now, thus says the Lord, who created you, O Jacob, and formed you, O Israel: Fear not for I have liberated you; I have called you by name, you are mine. When you pass through the water, I will be with you; in rivers you shall not drown. When you walk through fire, you shall not be burned; the flames shall not consume you. For I am the Lord, your God, the Holy One of Israel, your savior. I give Egypt and Seba in return for you. Because you are precious in my eyes and glorious, and because I love you.

Isaiah 43: 1-4a

It happened in those days that Jesus came from Nazareth of Galilee and was baptized in the Jordan by John. On coming up out of the water he saw the heavens being torn open and the Spirit, like a dove, descending upon him. And a voice came from the heavens proclaiming, "You are my beloved Son; with you I am well pleased."

Mark 1: 1-9

SPIRITUAL PRACTICE

You are invited to explore the unconditional and unmerited qualities of Divine Love. Take a few minutes to read through the scripture passages on the previous page. Insert your own name into the spaces where a name is indicated (Jacob, Israel, Jesus). Re-read these passages slowly and prayerfully as if they are a love letter written to you from your Divine Source. Allow the love letter to really sink into your being. Take 15-20 minutes with this activity. Record your reflections in the space provided.

YOU ARE LOVED

Fear	I am not loved
Compulsion	Envy
Sacred Truth	God is love and you are made of this love. This love cannot be denied, nor does it need to be earned – it is your very being.
Chakra	Heart

How we experience this fear being indulged

Emotions	Grief, sadness, despondency
Behavior	Withdrawing, difficulty trusting, lack of compassion or empathy, anger and resentment (used as a self-defense mechanism), victim behavior (poor me!).
Physical	Heart or lung problems, high blood pressure, asthma, problems in the arms or hands, immune system (thymus)
Element	Air

Evidence of healing

Inner State	Love, compassion, joy, mercy
Virtue	Mercy
Grace	Joy

QUESTIONS FOR FURTHER REFLECTION

❶ Do you believe that you are loved unconditionally? Do you love yourself without condition? If not, why not?

❷ How is this perception of a lack of unconditional love currently manifest in your life (high blood pressure, asthma, heart or lung disease, disease or injury in the arms or hands, susceptibility to upper respiratory disease (bronchitis, sinus infections, pneumonia, etc.)?

❸ What benefit(s) do you receive from not believing that you are loved unconditionally? What benefit(s) do you receive from not loving yourself unconditionally? (ie: "It allows me to receive sympathy from others.")

❹ How would your life change if you were able to believe that you do not need to earn love but that you are loved without condition? How would your life change if you were able to love yourself unconditionally?

❺ Why wouldn't you decide TODAY to embrace unconditional love of yourself?

❻ What do you need RIGHT NOW to believe this truth? Ask your higher power RIGHT NOW to help you to receive that which you perceive you will need in order to believe the truth of unconditional self-love. Write your request below.

SESSION SEVEN

Your Truth Shall Set You Free

The Fear	**I am not free to express my truth**
Compulsion	**Greed**
Truth	**The truth shall set you free!**

In the beginning was the Word, and the Word was with God, and the Word was God. The Word was in the beginning with God. All things came to be through The Word and without The Word, nothing came to be. What came to be through The Word was life and this life was the light of the human race; the light shines in the darkness and the darkness has not overcome it.

John 1: 1-5

People brought to him a deaf man who had a speech impediment and begged him to lay his hands on him. He took him off by himself away from the crowd. He put his finger into the man's ears and, spitting, touched his tongue; then he looked up to heaven and groaned and said to him, "Ephphatha!" (that is, "Be opened!") and immediately the man's ears were opened, his speech impediment was removed and he spoke plainly.

Mark 7: 32-35

You are the salt of the earth. But if salt loses its taste, with what can it be seasoned? It is no longer good for anything but to be thrown out and trampled underfoot. You are the light of the world. A city set on a mountain cannot be hidden. Nor do they light a lamp and then put it under a bushel basket; it is set on a lampstand, where it gives light to all in the house. Just so, your light must shine before others, that they may see your good deeds and glorify your heavenly Father.

Matthew 5: 13-16

SPIRITUAL PRACTICE

Part One: Scripture reflection

Prayerfully read through the scripture passages on the previous page. How are these passages speaking to you about your own tendency to withhold your gifts, your truth, your voice? What are the fears that are preventing you from expressing your truth and sharing your gifts? Write your reflections in the space provided.

Part Two: Sound Healing

One of the most effective means through which we are healed of the fear of expressing our truth is through the element of sound. For this meditation, you will need either a CD player and your favorite classical music CD or access to an internet music library (ie: YouTube, Rhapsody, Spotify, etc.) Create a calm and relaxing place where you can either sit comfortably or recline. Choose your favorite classical music piece or choose one from the suggestions below. Turn on the music and listen to it as loudly as you can tolerate. Allow yourself to relax into the music, paying attention to the movement of the sound along with any emotions that it may be triggering in you. Imagine as you are listening to the music that your fear of expressing your truth is being extracted and lifted up to the heavens for healing and release. If you are comfortable doing so, give your own voice to the sound, either through chanting AUM or AH along with the music. Below are some suggestions for music to be used. Record your thoughts and reflections in the space provided below and on the next page.

Music Suggestions:

Ave Maria; Schubert

Ave Maria; Bach

Air on a G-String; Bach

Concerto for Two Violins in D minor; Bach

Panis Angelicus; Franck

Ave Verum Corpus; Mozart

Hallelujah Chorus; Handel

YOUR TRUTH SHALL SET YOU FREE

Fear   I am not free to express my truth

Compulsion   Greed

Sacred Truth Expressing your truth shall set you free.

Chakra   Throat

How we experience this fear being indulged

Emotions   Restlessness, anger, anxiety, irritability, feeling of being insane or out of control.

Behaviors   Panic or anxiety attacks, withdrawal, depression, repression, problems communicating, expressing your needs.

Physical   Problems of the neck, shoulders, upper back, throat, mouth, teeth, thyroid, fibromyalgia.

Element   Sound

Evidence of healing

Inner state   Cohesive movement of ideas into reality

Virtue   Generosity

Grace   Freedom

QUESTIONS FOR FURTHER REFLECTION:

❶ Do you believe that you are free to fully and openly express your truth? If not, why not?

❷ How is this perception of an inability to openly and freely express your truth currently manifest in your life (neck or shoulder pain, hearing loss, throat or thyroid problems, fibromyalgia, etc.)

❸ What benefit(s) do you receive from not believing that you can speak your truth or withholding the gifts God has given you? (ie: It allows me to not have to face the challenge of change.)

❹ How would your life change if you were able to hear your truth and allow it to be expressed freely?

❺ Why wouldn't you decide TODAY to embrace your truth and give it expression?

❻ What do you need RIGHT NOW to believe this truth? Ask your higher power RIGHT NOW to help you to receive that which you perceive you will need in order to believe the truth of your ability to hear and give expression to your truth. Write your request below.

SESSION EIGHT

The Source of Knowledge Is Within

The Fear   **I am unable to see or know the truth**

Compulsion   **Sloth**

Truth   **The truth shall be revealed to you through your Divine Source (God). You need only open to Divine Guidance, perceive it and believe it!**

As Jesus walked along, he saw a man blind from birth. His disciples asked him, "Rabbi, who sinned, this man or his parents, that he was born blind?" Jesus answered, "Neither this man nor his parents sinned; he was born blind so that God's works might be revealed in him. We must perform the works of the one who sent me while it is day; night is coming when no one can work. As long as I am in the world, I am the light of the world."

When Jesus had said this, he spat on the ground and made mud with the saliva and spread the mud on the man's eyes, saying to him, "Go, wash in the pool of Siloam" (which means Sent). Then he went and washed and came back able to see.

The neighbors and those who had seen him before as a beggar began to ask, "Is this not the man who used to sit and beg?" Some were saying, "It is he." Others were saying, "No, but it is someone like him." He kept saying, "I am the man." But they kept asking him, "Then how were your eyes opened?" He answered, "The man called Jesus made mud, spread it on my eyes, and said to me, 'Go to Siloam and wash.' Then I went and washed and received my sight." They said to him, "Where is he?" He said, "I do not know."

They brought to the Pharisees the man who had formerly been blind. Now it was a Sabbath day when Jesus made the mud and opened his eyes. Then the Pharisees also began to ask him how he had received his sight. He said to them, "He put mud on my eyes. Then I washed, and now I see." Some of the Pharisees said, "This man is not from God, for he does not observe the Sabbath." But others said, "How can a man who is a sinner perform such signs?" And they were divided. So they said again to the blind man, "What do you say about him? It was your eyes he opened." He said, "He is a prophet."

The Judeans did not believe that he had been blind and had received his sight until they called the parents of the man who had received his sight and asked them, "Is this your son, who you say was born blind? How then does he now see?" His parents answered, "We know that this is our son, and that he was born blind; but we do not know how it is that now he sees, nor do we know who opened his eyes. Ask him; he is of age. He will speak for himself." His parents said this because they were afraid of the Judeans, who had already agreed that anyone who confessed Jesus to be the Messiah would be put out of the synagogue. Therefore, his parents said, "He is of age; ask him."

So for the second time, they called the man who had been blind, and they said to him, "Give Glory to God! We know that this man is a sinner." He answered, "I do not know whether he is a sinner. One thing I do know, that though I was blind, now I see." They said to him, "What did he do to you? How did he open your eyes?" He answered them, "I have told you already, and you would not listen. Why do you want to hear it again? Do you also want to become his disciples?" Then they reviled him, saying, "You are his disciple, but we are disciples of Moses. We know that God has spoken to Moses, but as for this person, we do not know where he comes from." The man answered, "Here is an astonishing thing! You do not know where he comes from, and yet he opened my eyes. We know that God does not listen to sinners, but does listen to anyone who is devout and obeys God's will. Never since the world began has it been heard that anyone opened the eyes of someone born blind. If this person were not from God, he could do nothing." They answered him, "You were born entirely in sin, and are you trying to teach us?" And they drove him out.

Jesus heard that they had driven him out, and when he found him, he said, "Do you believe in the Son-of-Man?" He answered, "And who is he, sir? Tell me, so that I may believe in him." Jesus said to him, "You have seen him, and he is the one speaking with you." He said, "Lord, I believe." And he worshiped Jesus. Jesus said, "I came into this world for judgment so that those who do not see may see, and those who do see may become blind." Some of the Pharisees near Jesus heard this and said to him, "Surely we are not blind, are we?" Jesus said to them, "If you were blind, you would not have sin. But now that you say, 'We see', your sin remains."

John 9: 1-41

SPIRITUAL PRACTICE

You are again invited to participate in an exercise in "Imagination/Contemplation". Read through the scripture passage slowly and prayerfully. Choose a character from the scripture and re-read the passage, imagining that you are that character. Then enter into the practice of Imagination/Contemplation, imagining the scene in its entirety with you being the character you have chosen. Imagine the scenery, the smells, the weather, etc. Really allow yourself to enter fully into the scene, allowing the story to unfold. Record your reflections in the space provided.

YOU DO KNOW

Fear   I do not know

Compulsion   Sloth

Sacred Truth   All wisdom, knowledge and truth are available to you through God.

Chakra   Brow

How we experience this fear being indulged

Emotions   Confusion, laziness, lack of motivation, not wanting to accept responsibility.

Behavior   Deferring to "perceived" authority rather than taking responsibility for discerning our own truth. Lack of faith/belief. Ignorance, prejudice, racism, judgmental behavior, discrimination, legalistic behavior, rigidity, believing you (or someone else) have the absolute truth. Believing that there is such a thing as absolute truth.

Physical   Headaches, eye issues, dizziness

Element   Light

Evidence of healing

Inner State   Openness to seeing and believing the truth as it is revealed to you and taking responsibility for it.

Virtue   Zeal

Grace   Knowledge, understanding

QUESTIONS FOR FURTHER REFLECTION

❶ Do you believe that you are free to fully and openly see and embrace your truth? If not, why not?

❷ How is this perception of an inability to openly and freely see your truth currently manifest in your life (vision problems, headaches, nightmares, mental confusion, obsessive thoughts, difficulty in learning or focusing, etc.)

❸ What benefit(s) do you receive from not believing that you can know or see your truth? (ie: "It allows me to remain ignorant, to not have to make a commitment to that truth.")

❹ How would your life change if you were able to see and know your truth?

❺ Why wouldn't you decide TODAY to embrace knowledge, wisdom and understanding?

❻ What do you need RIGHT NOW to believe this truth? Ask your higher power RIGHT NOW to help you to receive that which you perceive you will need in order to believe the truth of your ability to see and to know your truth. Write your request below.

SESSION NINE

You Are One With God

Fear	**I am alone**
Compulsion	**Pride**
Truth	**You are one with God and God with you and therefore with all there is.**

When you pray, go to your inner room, close the door and pray in secret. Your Divine Parent knows what you need before you ask.

Matthew 6: 1-8

Asked by the Pharisees when the kingdom of God would come, he said in reply, "The coming of the kingdom of God cannot be observed, and no one will announce, 'Look, here it is,' or 'There it is.' For behold, the kingdom of God is within you."

Luke 17: 20-21

Jesus, though he was in the form of God, did not regard equality with God something to be grasped. Rather, he emptied himself, taking the form of a slave, coming in human likeness; and found human in appearance, he humbled himself, becoming obedient to death, even death on a cross.

Philippians 2: 6-8

SPIRITUAL PRACTICE

You are invited to participate in an experience of Contemplative Prayer. In this prayer form, you are invited to rest in silence. Before you begin, you are encouraged to choose a word or image that you can use as your focus. Some choose an image of Jesus or the Buddha, or a word, such as Peace, Love or Joy. Choose a meditation posture that is comfortable for you: sitting upright with feet on the floor, sitting in the lotus position, or even lying down. Enter into the silence. Allow your brain to rest, not thinking, or worrying or going over the thoughts or stresses of the day. As you find your mind wandering (and you will!) go to your focus image or word, allowing that word or image to bring you back to the silence. Practice this form of meditation/prayer for 30 minutes, allowing yourself to open to the Divine Presence within you. Record any reflections in the space provided.

YOU ARE ONE WITH GOD

Fear   I am alone

Compulsion   Pride

Sacred Truth You are one with God and therefore never alone.

Chakra   Crown

How we experience this fear being indulged

Emotions   Depression, alienation, confusion, boredom, apathy.

Behaviors   Arrogance, operating out of our ego, believing we can or have to do it alone.

Physical   Confusion, physical heaviness, feeling of being paralyzed, pituitary gland issues; cerebral cortex, central nervous system disorders.

Element   Consciousness

Evidence of healing

Inner State Detachment, cooperation, knowing and living in oneness with God and all of creation. Seeking and surrendering to Divine Guidance.

Virtue   Humility

Grace   Bliss/Wisdom

QUESTIONS FOR FURTHER REFLECTION

❶ Do you believe that you are one with God and with all that is? How can you begin to explore this possibility?

❷ How is this perception of separation currently manifest in your life (depression, emotional paralysis, headaches, anxiety, a deep feeling of longing or loneliness, etc.)?

❸ What benefit(s) do you receive from believing that you are separate from God, others, creation? (ie: "It allows me to be right and others wrong, it gives me the illusion of having control, I get to feel sorry for myself for being burdened.")

❹ How would your life change if you were able to remember your oneness with God?

❺ Why wouldn't you decide TODAY to embrace the truth of oneness?

❻ What do you need RIGHT NOW to believe this truth? Ask your higher power RIGHT NOW to help you to believe in oneness. Write your request below.

AFTERWORD

Discernment

> *Whenever a person turns to the Lord, the veil is removed. Now the Lord is the Spirit, and where the Spirit of the Lord is, there is freedom.*
> 2 Corinthians 16-17

FREEDOM

Freedom, understood from a spiritual perspective, is God's deepest desire for us and God's loving hand has planted the desire in our hearts to return to this state of freedom. This Divine desire compels, urges, provokes, inspires and guides (and nags, goads, tortures, taunts) us along the path to its realization. This divinely ordained freedom, known by its deep state of peace, joy and love, has nothing to do with our external circumstances, as it is, by its very nature, an internal quality. Divine freedom is expansive, life-giving and filled with growth and promise. When we are able to name and claim the truth that God reveals to us as our highest good, we enjoy the greatest expression of spiritual freedom. The process of authentic freedom provides the tools through which this freedom can be embraced and enjoyed. This journey, however, would not be complete without one critical tool for spiritual growth: *discernment*.

DISCERNMENT

Discernment is the informal or formal process through which we distinguish the voice of God from the voice of the false self or ego. The voice of God leads us toward freedom. The ego, on the other hand, is the voice of temptation trying to keep us from our Divinely ordained path. The ego, like the devil sitting on our shoulder, whispers guilt, fear, worry, wants and desires into our ears, tempting us away from the path of God. In contrast, God's voice is like the angel sitting on the opposite shoulder, inviting us to choose the path that is in our highest good. Discernment allows us to freely choose the path that will be uniquely in our highest good. The good news is that God makes the knowledge of this path available to all of us - if we only ask.

TOOLS OF DISCERNMENT

Meditation and prayer are the vehicles through which we enter into this process of discernment, as are observation and support through our Spiritual Director, Counselor or close spiritual friends. Discernment allows us to hear the voice of God more clearly and to recognize the voice of the ego which strives to imprison us in the status quo.

TESTING DISCERNMENT

The ultimate test in the process of discernment is freedom - Does this path or choice give me peace, allow me to know love more fully, experience contentment and joy; is it expansive, life-giving and supportive?" If the answer to these questions is yes, then perhaps the path is being revealed to be "of God." If the answer is no, then perhaps what we have discerned is coming out of our fears, false perceptions, and ego attachments. Responding to the voice of God and stepping into the ever-expanding path of freedom, we are able to live more fully within the peace and compassion that is our original nature, while releasing the fears and ego attachments that hold us back.

FRUITS OF THE PROCESS

Entering into the process of Authentic Freedom with the support of sound discernment, the foundation is established upon which Divine freedom can take root and grow. As we grow spiritually and allow ourselves to be healed of our inner wounds, this is a process that can be returned to again and again in your desire to remember your true nature while embracing a profound and lasting peace.

Authentic Freedom – Claiming a Life of Contentment and Joy;
Lauri Ann Lumby; St. Johann Press; 2011

Appendix A - Your Energy Anatomy

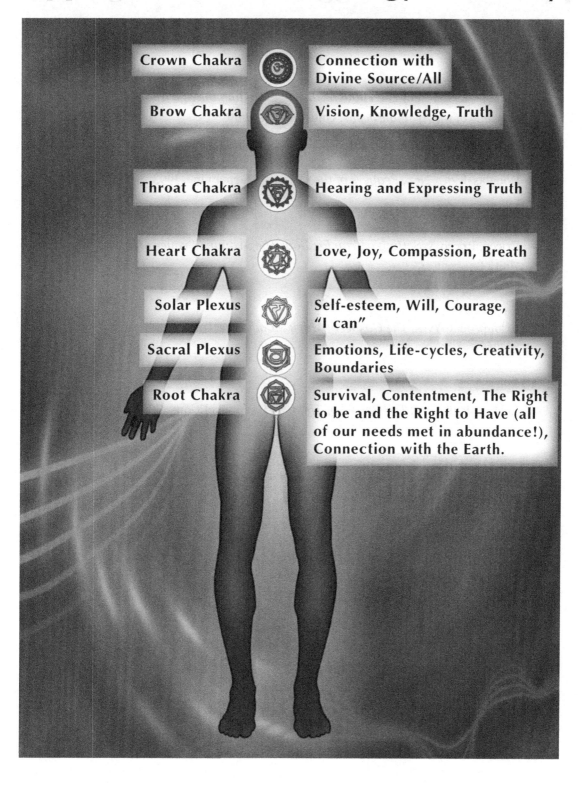

Crown Chakra — Connection with Divine Source/All

Brow Chakra — Vision, Knowledge, Truth

Throat Chakra — Hearing and Expressing Truth

Heart Chakra — Love, Joy, Compassion, Breath

Solar Plexus — Self-esteem, Will, Courage, "I can"

Sacral Plexus — Emotions, Life-cycles, Creativity, Boundaries

Root Chakra — Survival, Contentment, The Right to be and the Right to Have (all of our needs met in abundance!), Connection with the Earth.

Appendix B - Suggested Reading

Douglas-Klotz, Neil, *The Hidden Gospel: Decoding the Spiritual Message of the Aramaic Jesus*, Quest Books, 1999

Douglas-Klotz, Neil, *Prayers of the Cosmos*, Harper One, 1993

Ericco, Rocco A. *Setting a Trap for God: The Aramaic Prayer of Jesus*, Unity Books, 1997

Leloup, Jean-Yves, *The Gospel of Mary Magdalene*, Inner Traditions, 2002

Leloup, Jean-Yves, *The Gospel of Thomas*, Inner Traditions, 2005

Ramsay, Jay, *The Crucible of Love: The Path to Passionate and True Relationships*, O Books, 2005

Schwan, Marie, Syrup-Bergin, Jacqueline, *Love: A Guide for Prayer*, Word Among Us Press, 2004

Kubler-Ross, Elizabeth, *On Death and Dying*, Scribner Classics, 1997

Judith, Anodea, *Wheels of Life: A User's Guide to the Chakra System*, Llewellyn Publications, 1987

Myss, Caroline, *Anatomy of the Spirit: The Seven Stages of Power and Healing*, Three Rivers Press, 1997

Mirdad, Michael, *The Seven Initiations of the Spiritual Path*, A.R.E. Press, 2004

Levine, Peter A., *Waking the Tiger: Healing Trauma*, North Atlantic Books, 1997

Servan-Schreiber, M.D., PhD, David, *The Instinct to Heal: Curing Depression, Anxiety and Stress without Drugs and without Talk Therapy*, Rodale Books, 2004

Lauri Lumby is the creator of Authentic Freedom and its companion programs in spiritual formation for adults. Lauri is a trained Spiritual Director, Hands-on Healer and Lay Minister. She has worked in the field of Pastoral Ministry since 1994 and is the owner of Authentic Freedom Ministries in Oshkosh, Wisconsin. You can contact Lauri through her website: www.yourspiritualtruth.com

Made in the USA
Monee, IL
12 March 2024